The original

ŠEVČÍK

VIOLIN STUDIES

STUDIES PREPARATORY TO THE SHAKE & DEVELOPMENT IN DOUBLE-STOPPING

TRILLER-VORSTUDIEN

EXERCICES POUR PRÉPARER ET DÉVELOPPER LE TRILLE

Op. 7 Part 2

BOSWORTH

Triller-Uebungen
in der 2. **3. 4. 5.** 6. Lage.
ESERCIZI SUL TRILLO
nella 2ᵃ 3ᵃ 4ᵃ 5ᵃ e 6ᵃ posizione.

Traduzione italiana di M. PÉLISSIER

Exercices de trille
dans la 2ᵉ, 3ᵉ, 4ᵉ, 5ᵉ et 6ᵉ position.

Trilková cvičení v **2. 3. 4. 5.** a 6. poloze.

Trill exercises
in the **2. 3. 4. 5** and 6 positions.

Упражненія въ трели во 2ᵒй, 3ей, 4ой, 5ой и 6ой позиціяхъ.

1.

2. Lage.
2ᵃ posizione.

2. Position.
2. poloha.

2ая позиція.

Edited by H. Brett.

B. & Co 4290

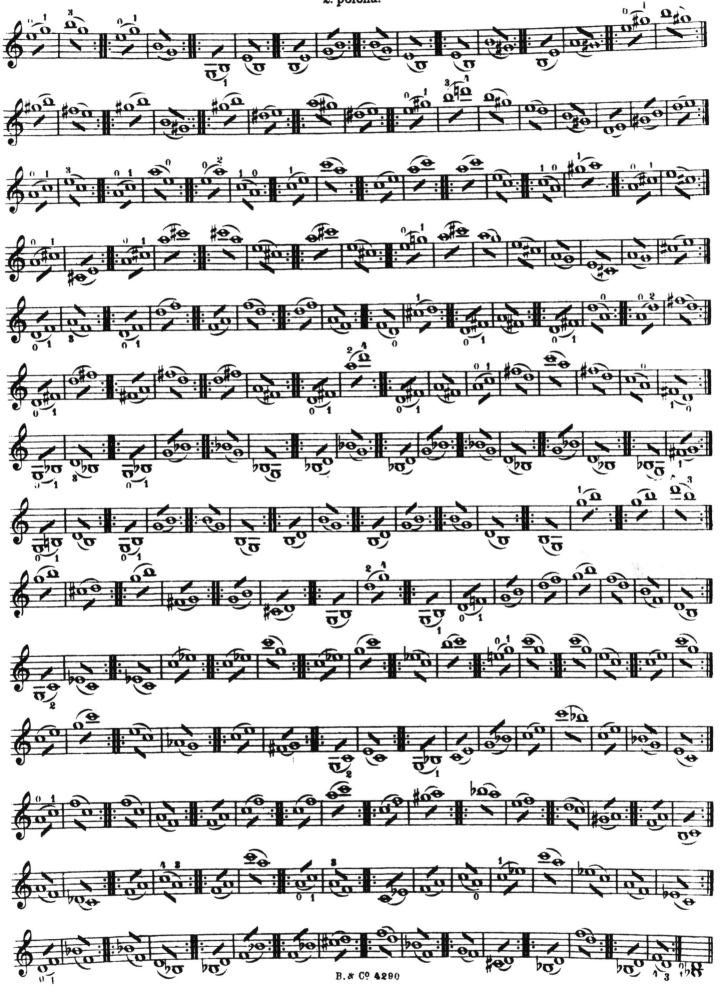

2.

3.

3ª posizione.   **3. Position.**   3ья позиція.
8. poloha.

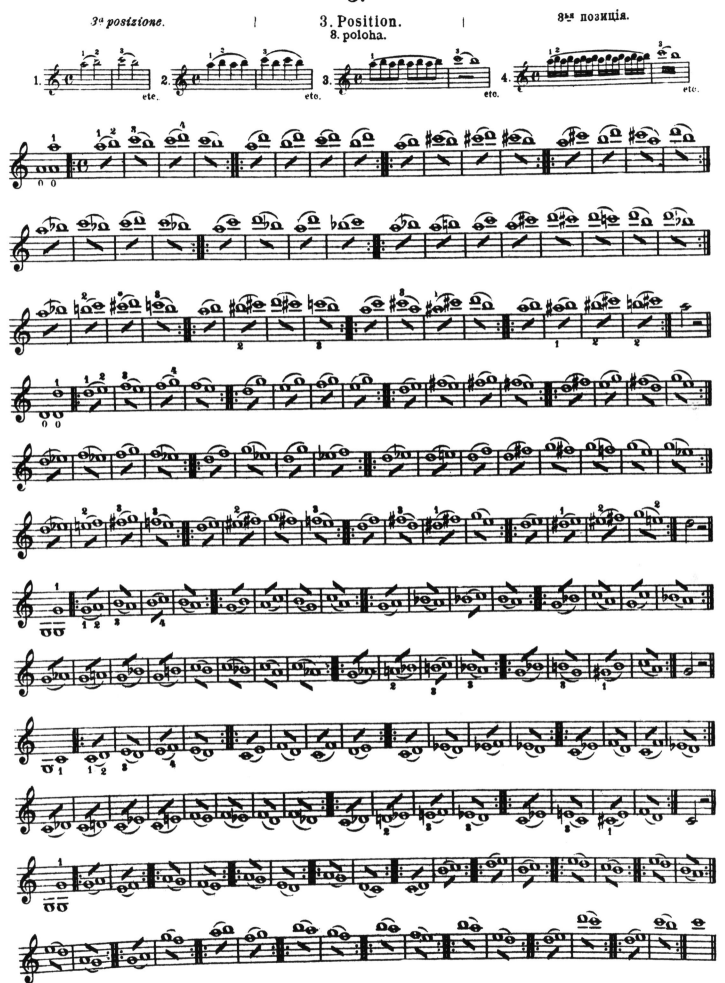

3ᵉ poststone. **3. Position.** 8ᵗ⁹ позиція.
8. poloha.

4.

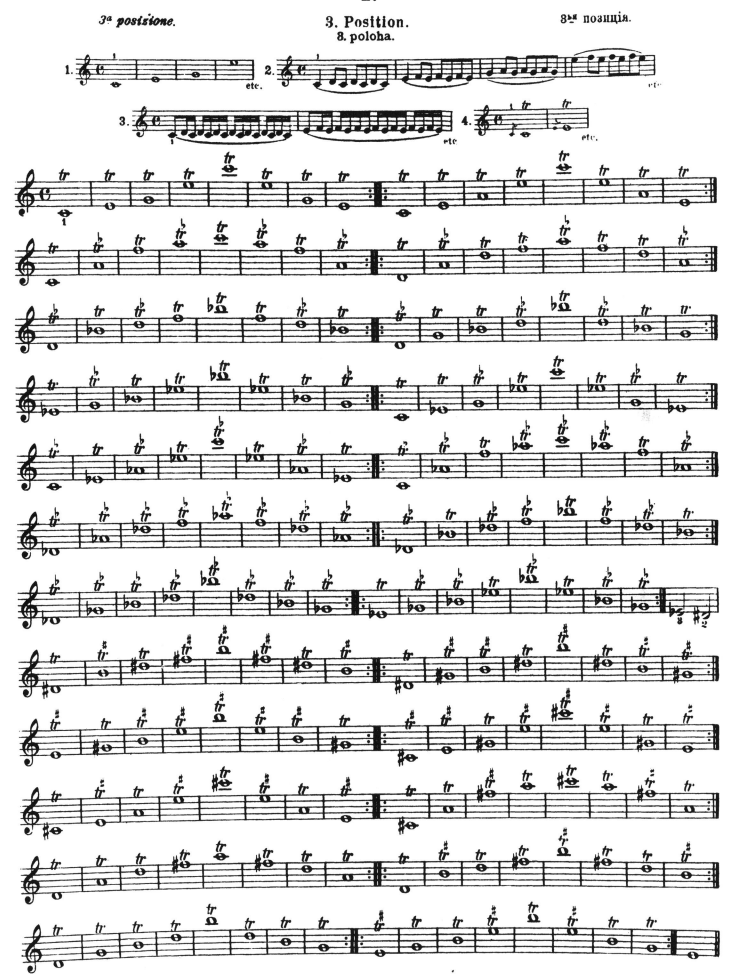

8

5.

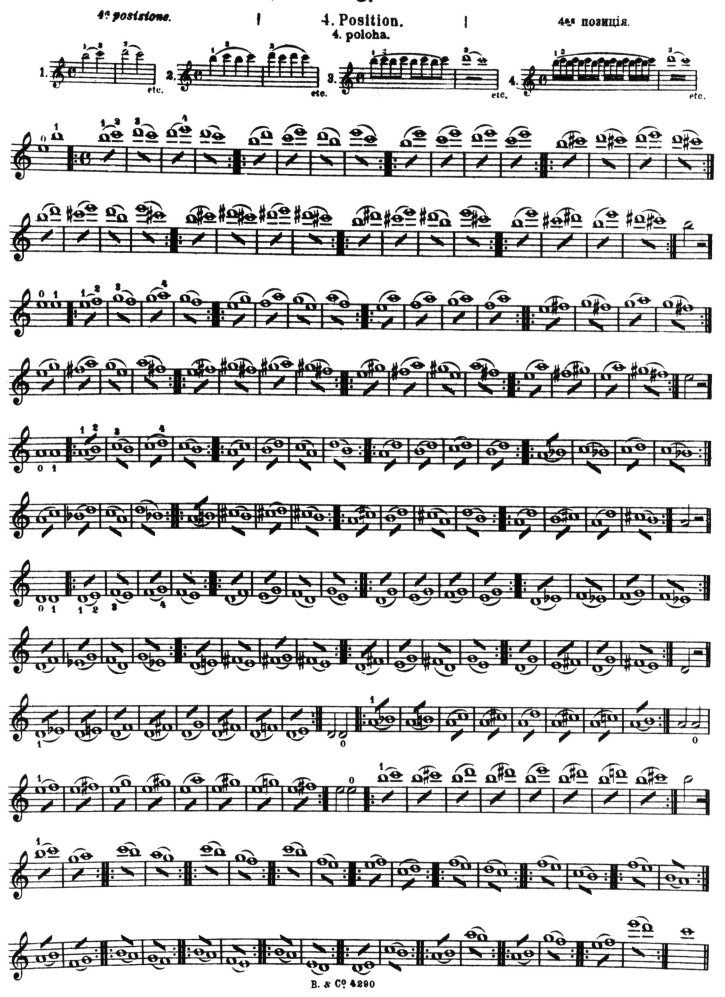

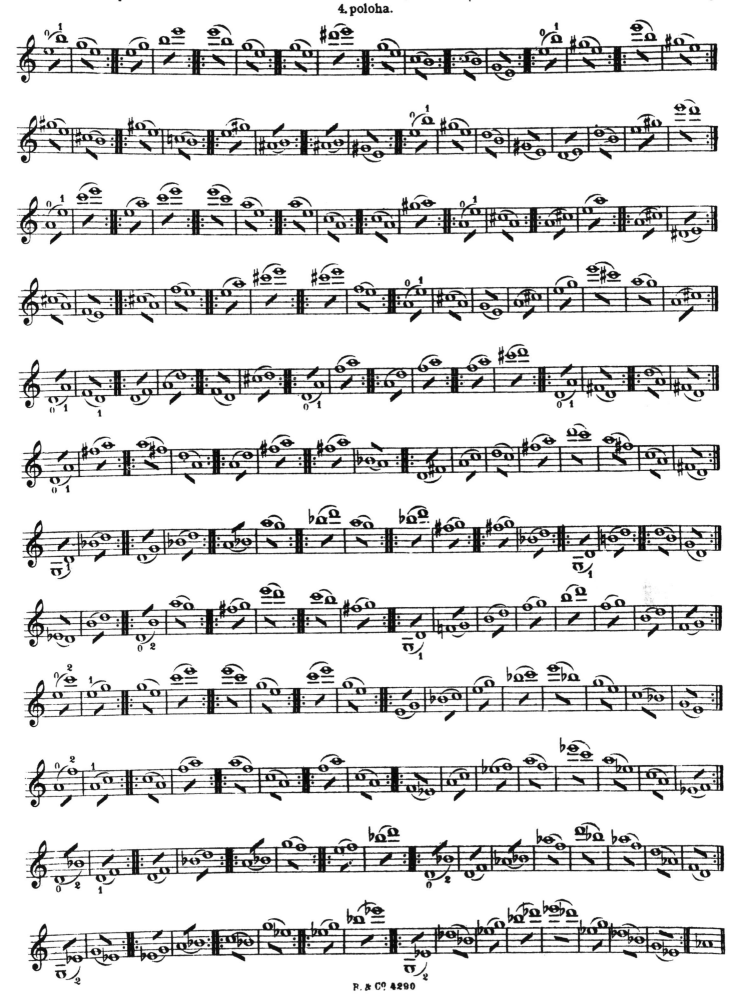

6.

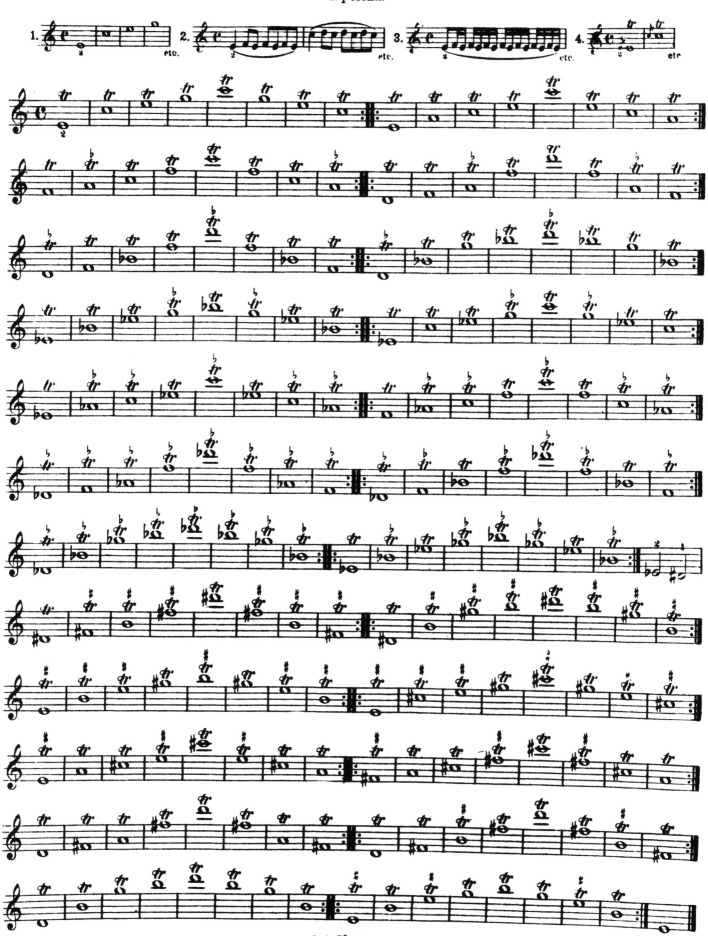

7.

8.

5ª positione.   5. Position. 5. poloha.   5ая позиція.

5. Position.
5. poloha.

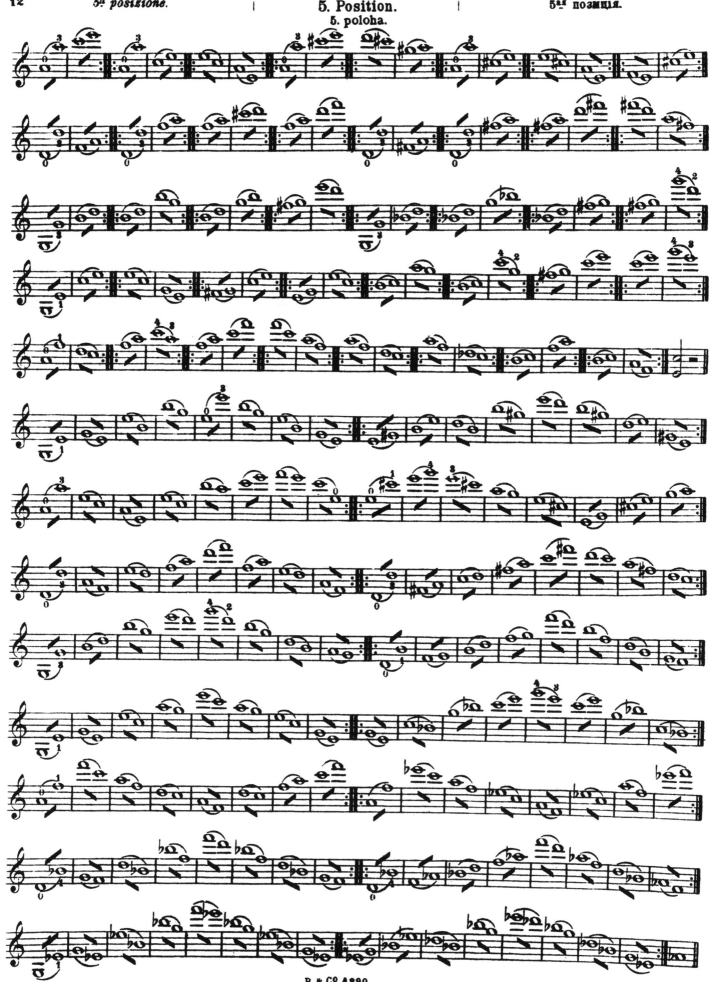

9.

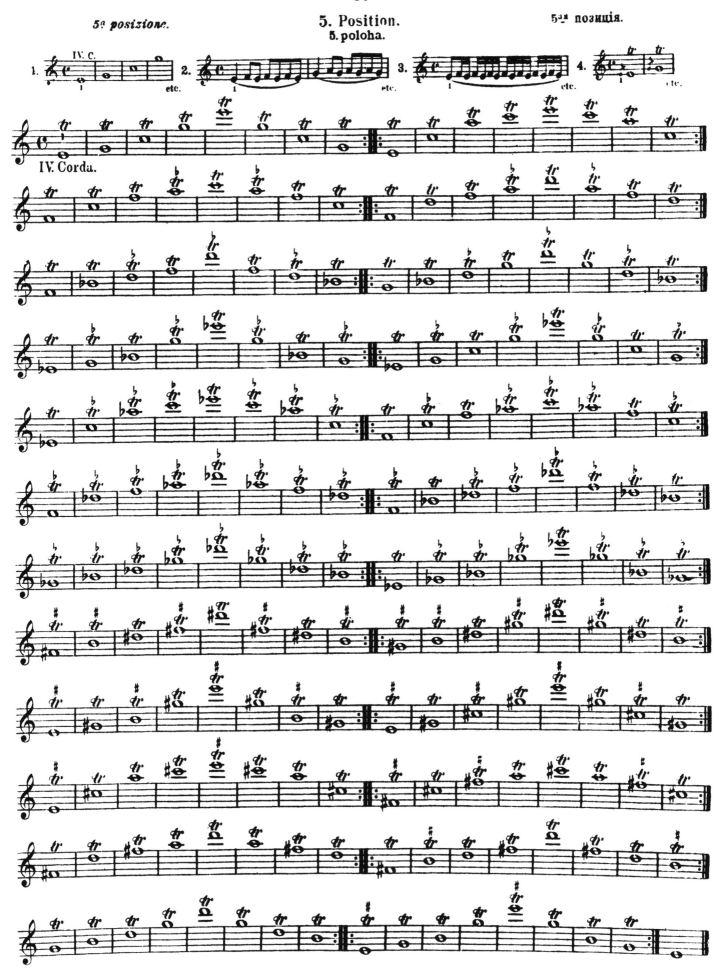

14

10.

11.

12.

13.

14.

4ª *posizione*.

4. Position.
4. poloha.

4ᵃᵃ позиція.

15.

4ᵃ *posizione.*   4. Position.   4ая позиція.
4. poloha.

16.

5. Position.

5. poloha.

5ª posizione.

5ая позиція.

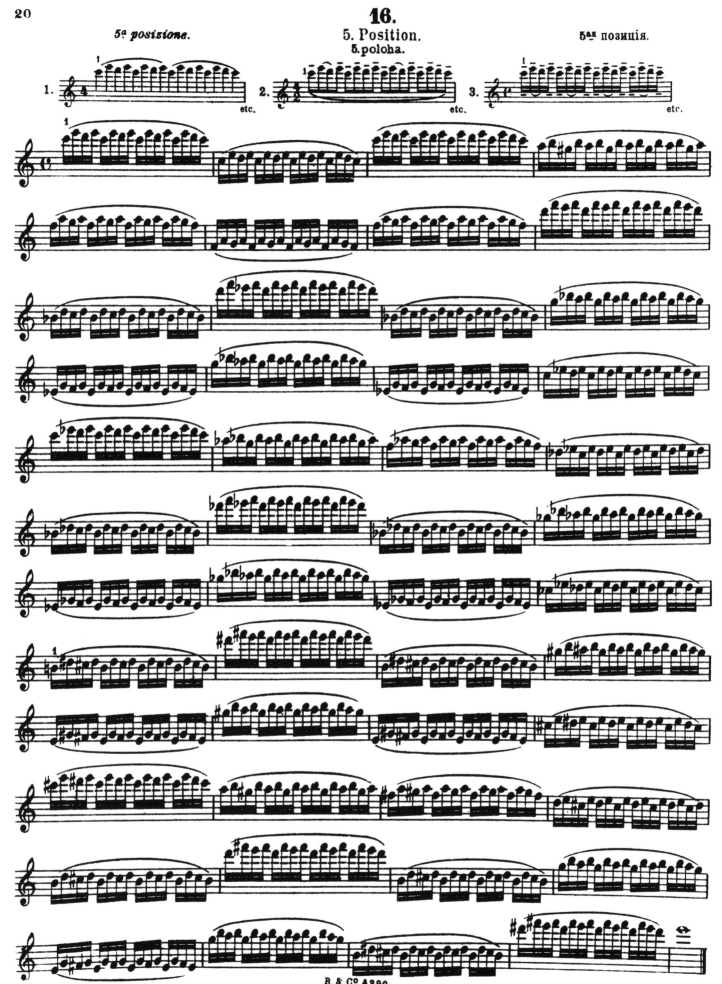

17.

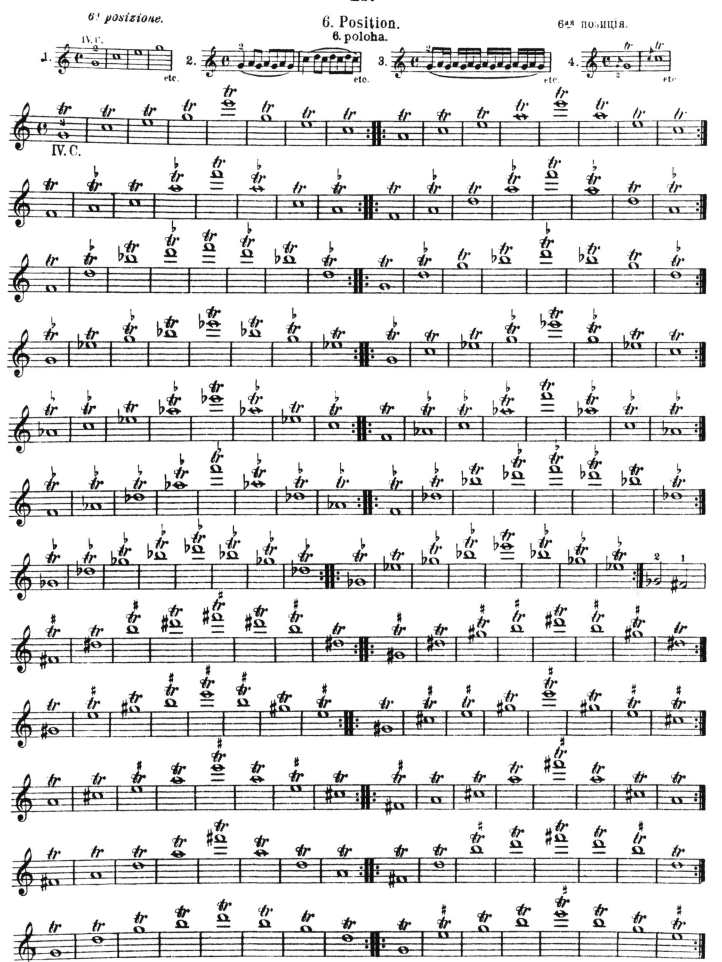

18.

19.

1ª - 3ª posizione.

1.- 3. Position.
1.- 8. poloha.

1-8 позиція.

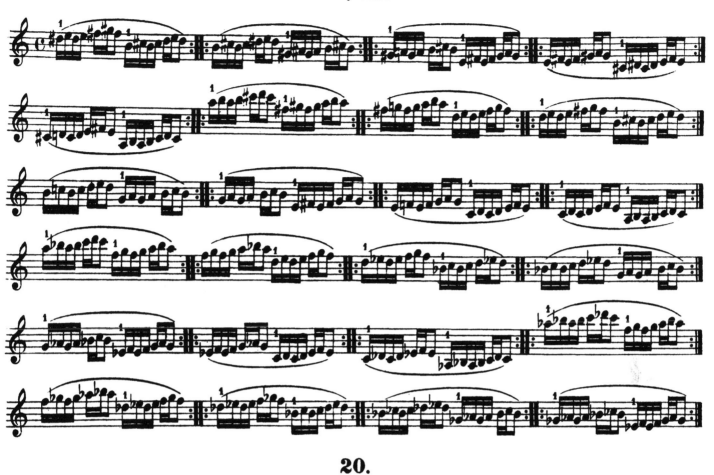

20.

1ª - 3ª posizione.

1.- 3. Position.
1.- 8. poloha.

1-8 позиція.

24.

25.

3 posizione.

3. Position.
8. poloha.

3ья позиція.

26.

4ª positione. **4. Position.** 4. poloha. 4ᵃᵈ позиція.

27.

2ª posizione. **2. Position.** 2ᵃᵃ позиція.
2. poloha.

28.

3. Position.

8. poloha..

3ª posizione.

8ᵃ позиція..

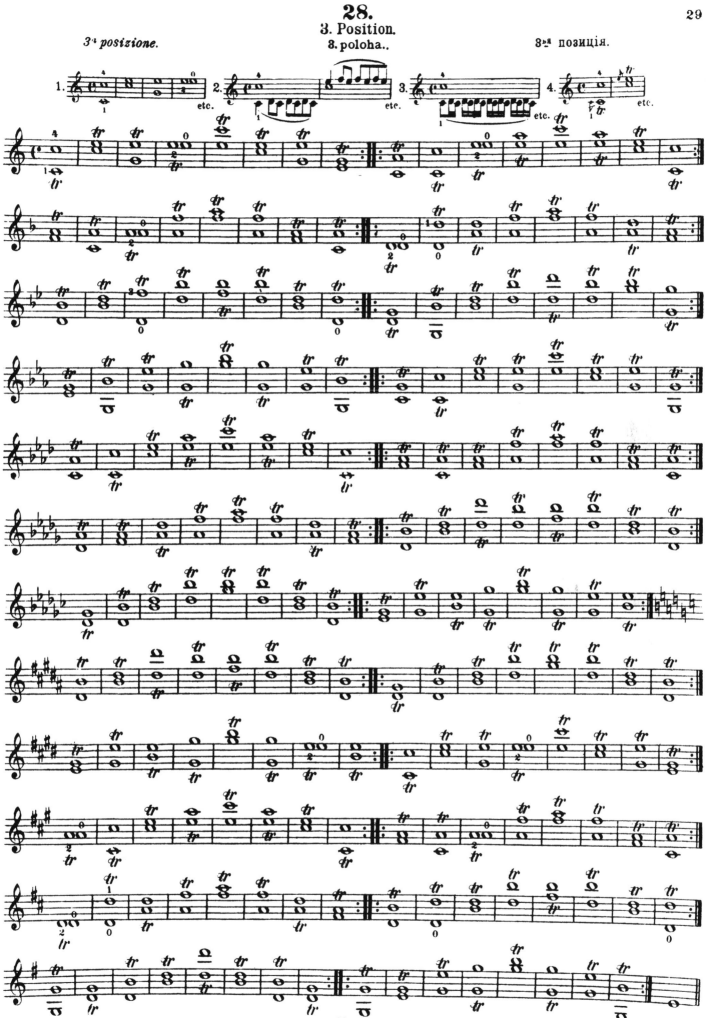

DANCE MUSIC FROM OLD VIENNA
(Tanzmusik aus Alt-Wien)

2 Violins, Guitar, Bass & Clarinet

H a y d n Josef			Zingarese Nr. 1, 6, 8

2 Violins, Viola, Bass, Flute, Clarinet & 2 Horns

B e e t h o v e n Ludwig			6 Kontratänze
H a y d n Josef			Katharinen-Tänze
			Nr. 4, 6, 8, 12
L a n n e r Josef	op.	16	Bruder Halt, Galopp
	op.	82	Jägers Lust, Galopp
	op.	93	Pesther Walzer
	op.	148	Malapou-Galopp
	op.	194	Hansjörgel-Polka
			2 Mazurka
M o z a r t W.A.			3 Kontratänze K.V. 462
			4 Deutsche Tänze
			K.V. 586, 600, 606
S c h u b e r t Franz	op.	49	Ecossaisen DV. 299
S t r a u s s Johann	op.	9	Seufzer-Galopp
(Vater)	op.	90	Jugendfeuer-Galopp
	op.	137	Annen-Polka
S t r a u s s Johann	op.	202	Eisele u. Beisele Sprünge
(Sohn)	op.	72	Scherz-Polka
S t r a u s s Josef	op.	214	Marienklänge, Walzer

3 Violins & Bass

L a n n e r Josef	op.	1	Neue Wiener Ländler
	op.	145	Marien-Walzer
	op.	180	Abendsterne-Walzer

2 Violins, Viola & Bass

K r u s c h n i k Lucas			2 Alt-Wiener Miniaturen
			(Harfe & Klavier a.l.)
L a n n e r Josef	op.	103	Die Werber, Walzer
	op.	163	Steyrische Tänze
	op.	189	Cerrita-Polka
P a y e r Hieronimus			Galanterie-Walzer
S c h u b e r t Franz			Walzer und Ländler aus
			DV. 9, 18, 67, 77. 127
			Deutsche Tänze und Walzer aus
			DV. 145, 366, 796, 790
S t r a u s s Johann	op.	6	Kettenbrücke, Walzer
	op.	51	Hofballtänze, Walzer
(Vater)	op.	101	Salon-Polka
	op.	116	Wiener Gemüts-Walzer
	op.	249	Exeter-Polka
S t r a u s s Josef	op.	26	Die guten alten Zeiten
(Vater)	op.	53	Bajaderen-Walzer

2 Violins & Guitar

M a y e r Johann			Schnofler Tanz
S t e l z m ü l l e r Vinzenz			Stelzmüller Tanz

STAGE FRIGHT

ITS CAUSES AND CURES

WITH SPECIAL REFERENCE TO VIOLIN PLAYING

BY

KATO HAVAS

===== CONTENTS =====

also by Kato Havas

A NEW APPROACH TO VIOLIN PLAYING
THE TWELVE LESSON COURSE
THE VIOLIN & I

STRING ORCHESTRA STREICHORCHESTER
ORCHESTRE A CORDES ORCHESTRA D'ARCHI

The following concertos and concertinos from the list are available with full string orchestral accompaniment:

Nachstehende Konzerte und Concertinos aus unserem Angebot sind mit voller Streichorchester-Begleitung lieferbar:

Les concertos et les concertinos de la liste suivante sont disponibles avec leur accompagnement d'orchestre à cordes:

I seguenti concerti e concertini come da lista sono disponibili con accompagnamento d'orchestra d'archi:

このリストにあるコンチェルトとコンチェルティノスは
すべて完全な ストリング・オーケストラの伴奏付きです。

* Kuchler	Opus 12	* Portnoff	Opus 13	Seitz	Opus 15
* Kuchler	Opus 15	Rieding	Opus 34	Seitz	Opus 22
* Millies	(In the style of Mozart)	* Rieding	Opus 35	Ten Have	Opus 30

SELECTED PIECES FROM HANDEL edited by Felix Borowski

AUSGEWÄHLTE STÜCKE VON HÄNDEL herausgegeben von Felix Borowski

PIECES CHOISIES DE HAENDEL éditées par Félix Borowski

SELEZIONI DI PEZZI DI HÄNDEL curate da Felix Borowski

ヘンデル小品集 フェリックス・ボロウスキ 校閲

Bourree   Gavotte   Hornpipe   Largo   Menuet   Musette   Sarabande

*SIX VERY EASY PIECES in the First Position by Edward Elgar

*SECHS SEHR LEICHTE STÜCKE in der Ersten Lage von Edward Elgar

*SIX PIECES TRES FACILES dans la Première Position d'Edward Elgar

*SEI PEZZI MOLTO FACILI in Prima Posizione di Edward Elgar

* やさしい小品 6曲集 ファースト・ポジション エドワード・エルガー 校閲

All these are available with Piano, 1st Violin, 2nd Violin, 3rd Elementary Violin, 4th Violin (in lieu of Viola), Viola, 'Cello and Double Bass.
   * Also with additional parts for woodwind, brass and percussion.

Alle angeführten Werke lieferbar mit Klavier, 1. Violine, 2. Violine, 3. Violine (Obligat), 4. Violine (an Stelle von Viola), Viola, 'Cello und Kontrabaß.
   * auch mit zusätzlichen Stimmen für Holzblasinstrumente, Blechbläser und Schlagzeug.

Tous sont disponibles avec piano, 1er violon, 2ème violon, 3ème violon (élémentaire), 4ème violon (à la place de l'alto), alto, violoncelle et contrebasse.
   * Disponibles aussi avec les parties supplémentaires de bois, cuivres et percussions.

Tutti questi pezzi sono disponibili per pianoforte, primo violino, secondo violino, terzo violino semplice, quarto violino (al posto della viola), viola, violoncello e contrabasso.
   * anche con parti aggiuntive per strumenti a fiato, ottoni e strumenti a percussione.

これらは すべて、ピアノ、第1バイオリン、第2バイオリン、
第3エリメンタリー・バイオリン、第4バイオリン、ビオラ、
チェロ、ダブルベース のパート付きです。

   * ウッドウインド、ブラス、パーカッションのパートもあります。

BOSWORTH